# It's My State! ★ ★ ★ ★ ★

# HAWAII

## The Aloha State

Steven Otfinoski, Ann Graham Gaines, and
Jacqueline Laks Gorman

Cavendish
Square

New York

Published in 2016 by Cavendish Square Publishing, LLC
243 5th Avenue, Suite 136, New York, NY 10016

Third Edition

Website: cavendishsq.com

CPSIA Compliance Information: Batch #WS15CSQ

All websites were available and accurate when this book was sent to press.

Library of Congress Cataloging-in-Publication Data

Otfinoski, Steven.
Hawaii / Steven Otfinoski, Ann Graham Gaines, and Jacqueline Laks Gorman.
pages cm. — (It's my state!) (A quick look at Hawaii — The Aloha State — From the beginning — The people — How the government works — Making a living.)
Includes bibliographical references and index.
ISBN 978-1-62713-157-5 (hardcover) ISBN 978-1-62713-159-9 (ebook)
1. Hawaii—Juvenile literature. I. Gaines, Ann. II. Gorman, Jacqueline Laks, 1955- III. Title.

DU623.25.O85 2016
996.9—dc23

2014049273

Editorial Director: David McNamara
Editor: Fletcher Doyle
Copy Editor: Rebecca Rohan
Art Director: Jeffrey Talbot
Designer: Alan Sliwinski
Senior Production Manager: Jennifer Ryder-Talbot
Production Editor: Renni Johnson
Photo Research: J8 Media

The photographs in this book are used by permission and through the courtesy of: Justinreznick/Getty Images, cover; Terry Smith Images/Alamy, 4; David L. Moore/Alamy, 4; Daniel Ramirez/File:Kukui Fruit – Hoomaluhia Botanical Garden.jpg/Wikimedia Commons, 4; Steven Maltby/Shutterstock.com, 5; Stephen Frink Collection/Alamy, 5; Photo Resource Hawaii/Alamy, 5; tobkatrina/Shutterstock.com, 6; Jacques Jangoux/Alamy, 8; Douglas Peebles Photography/Alamy, 9; Westgraphix LLC, 10; Dennis Frates/Alamy, 11; Rick Strange/Alamy, 12; John Elk III/Alamy, 13; aijohn784/iStock Editorial/Thinkstock, 14; Maridav/Shutterstock.com, 14; Alberto Loyo/Shutterstock.com, 14; Lisa Hoang/Shutterstock.com, 15; Ann Cecil/Lonely Planet Images/Getty Images, 15; Joe West/Shutterstock.com, 15; Lazlo Podor/Alamy, 16; Douglas Peebles Photography/Alamy, 17; Photo Resource Hawaii/Alamy, 18; Pacific Stock/Superstock, 19; AP Photo/Brookfield Zoo, Jim Schultz, 20; AP Photo/Jim Collins, 20; Photo Resource Hawaii/Alamy, 20; CHAIYA/Shutterstock.com, 21; Archiwiz/Shutterstock.com, 21; WaterFrame/Alamy, 21; Phil Walter/Getty Images, 22; Pacific Stock/Superstock, 24; Classic Image/Alamy, 25; Mauro Ladu/Alamy, 26; John Elk III/Alamy, 29; Photo Resource Hawaii/Alamy, 30; Historical Collection/Corbis, 31; Hawaiian Legacy Archive/Perspectives/Getty Images, 32; Toni Salama/Chicago Tribune/MCT/Getty Images, 34; cleanfotos/Shutterstock.com, 34; Daderot/File:Ho'omaluhia Botanical Garden - mountain view.JPG/Wikimedia Commons, 34; Lonely Planet/Lonely Planet Images/getty Images, 34; AP Photo/PBS, 36; North Wind Picture Archives/Alamy, 38; AP Photo, 39; Greg Vaughn/Alamy, 40; AP Photo/Marco Garcia, 41; EpicStockMedia/Shutterstock.com, 44; Debra Behr/Alamy, 47; Daniel DeSlover/Shutterstock.com, 48; Brian A. Witkin/Shutterstock.com, 48; Jaguar PS/Shutterstock.com, 48; North Wind Picture Archives, 49; Tim Mosenfelder/Getty Images, 49; AP Photo/Scott A. Miller, 49; Photo Resource Hawaii/Alamy, 50; Accurate Art, 50; John Oeth/Alamy, 52; Alan C. Heison/Shutterstock.com, 54; Karl Lehmann/Lonely Planet Images/Getty Images, 54; Photo Resource Hawaii/Alamy, 55; Lonely Planet Images/Alamy, 55; blahedo/File:Statue of Father Damien 3.jpeg/Wikimedia Commons, 56; Kerry Gershaneck/File:Hawaii State Legislature.jpg/Wikimedia Commons, 58; David Moore—Oahu/Alamy, 59; AFP/Getty Images, 61; AP Photo/The Advertiser, Bruce Asato, 62; Marco Garcia/Getty Images, 62; AP Photo/Jae C. Hong, 62; AP Photo/Parson USN/UXB Joint Venture, 63; Deborah Kolb/Shutterstock.com, 64; Pacific Stock/Superstock, 66; Craig Ellenwood/Alamy, 67; JTB Photo/Superstock, 68; Pacific Stock/Superstock, 68; Ron Dahlquist/Superstock, 69; Flirt/Superstock, 69; Olyina/Shutterstock.com, 70; Specialist Stock/Corbis, 72; CBS/Getty Images, 73; Christopher Santoro, 74; Caleb Foster/Shutterstock.com, 75; Joe West/Shutterstock.com, 75; Christopher Santoro (flag and seal), 76.

Printed in the United States of America

# HAWAII

★ ★ ★ ★

# CONTENTS

# A QUICK LOOK AT
## STATEHOOD: AUGUST 21, 1959

### ★ State Bird: Nene

The nene (pronounced nay-nay), or Hawaiian goose, is a black and gray goose that lives only in Hawaii. Unlike all other geese, the nene does not live near water. Most nene live on the slopes of the Mauna Kea and Mauna Loa volcanoes, on the Big Island of Hawaii.

### ★ State Flower: Hibiscus

In 1988, Hawaii's state legislature declared the yellow hibiscus as the official state flower. Hibiscus flowers can come in a range of colors, including white, red, or pink. These striking flowers attract butterflies and hummingbirds.

### ★ State Tree: Kukui

The kukui, or candlenut tree, was brought to Hawaii by **Polynesian** settlers more than a thousand years ago. The early Hawaiians placed the oil-rich nuts in stone lamps or torches and lit them. They also used kukui wood to build canoes. The kukui was chosen as Hawaii's official state tree in 1959.

# HAWAII
## POPULATION: 1,360,301

### ★ State Gem: Black Coral

Black coral are tiny marine animals that live in colonies (groups) in tropical oceans. Black coral can be found in shady, shallow water and deep in underwater caves. Early Hawaiians harvested the skeletons of black coral to use as charms and to make medicine. Today, black coral is often used in jewelry.

### ★ State Marine Mammal: Humpback Whale

Female humpback whales, which are larger than males, can grow to be about 45 feet (14 meters) long. Every winter, thousands of humpbacks migrate from the waters off Alaska to the oceans around the Hawaiian Islands. There, they breed, give birth, and care for their young. The federal government established the Hawaiian Islands Humpback Whale National Marine Sanctuary in 1992.

### ★ State Dance: Hula

Hula has been performed in Hawaii since Polynesian people arrived at the islands. Hula dancers honored their gods and rulers. Today, there are two types of hula. Traditional dances are performed to chanted poetry and are often accompanied by drumming. Modern hula dances are performed to music from steel guitars, ukuleles, and drums.

Heavy rainfall makes the vegetation on Kauai green and thick.

# The Aloha State

The state of Hawaii is located in the middle of the Pacific Ocean. The state is north of the equator. Hawaii is made up of an **archipelago**, or chain of islands. Because it is surrounded by so much water, the Hawaiian archipelago is the most isolated population center on Earth.

California lies about 2,390 miles (3,850 kilometers) to the east of Hawaii, and Japan is almost 4,000 miles (6,400 km) to the west. In the past, it took weeks to reach Hawaii in a sailing ship. Today, it takes travelers from California less than six hours to get to Hawaii by airplane. Many people consider Hawaii a paradise because of its remote location and its incredible natural beauty. Because Hawaii is an island state, residents refer to the rest of the United States (except for Alaska) as the mainland. To Hawaiians, the mainland includes the forty-eight contiguous, or connected, states on the North American continent.

## A Chain of Islands

If you look at most maps of the state of Hawaii, you will see only eight islands. In fact, the state covers the entire Hawaiian archipelago, which includes 132 islands, reefs, and shoals (sandy elevations), many of which are tiny, with areas of less than 50 acres (20 hectares). Although Hawaii is far from being the world's largest archipelago, it is still quite long.

Cliffs on the Napali Coast drop into the ocean at the northwest shore of Kauai.

The Hawaiian archipelago stretches over a distance of more than 1,500 miles (2,400 km). In terms of land area, Hawaii is made up of only 6,423 square miles (16,635 square kilometers), which makes it one of the smallest states. But the state also includes another 4,500 square miles (11,650 sq km) of water—found in the islands' many bays and inlets, and in some of the surrounding ocean waters.

Hawaii's eight main islands are clustered at the southeastern end of the Hawaiian archipelago. Going from the southeast to the northwest, they are Hawaii (also called the Big Island), Maui, Kahoolawe, Lanai, Molokai, Oahu, Kauai, and Niihau. People live on just seven of these eight islands since Kahoolawe is now abandoned. During and after World War II (1939–1945), the US Navy used Kahoolawe to practice bombing exercises. Although this practice ended in 1990, the island still has no permanent residents.

## Volcanic Origins

The Hawaiian Islands are actually the tops of volcanoes. The bottoms of these volcanoes sit on the ocean floor. The land that lies above the waves is considered an island.

According to **geologists**, scientists who study Earth's structure and history, Earth's surface is broken up into huge pieces called plates. These plates move slowly. Over the years, they bump together. When the pressure gets too strong, one plate jolts past or under the other, causing earthquakes. Hawaii sits in the middle of a plate in the Pacific Ocean. Many millions of years ago, this Pacific Plate began to slowly pass over what is called a hot spot. At the hot spot, **magma**—hot, melted rock—bubbled up through Earth's crust and formed the Hawaiian volcanoes, one by one. (When magma reaches the surface, it is called lava.) Slowly, each of the volcanoes moved off the hot spot, and over time the volcanoes formed a long chain.

Kilauea is called the world's most active volcano. It is located on the island of Hawaii.

The oldest volcanoes, located at the northern end of the chain, have now sunk beneath the waves. Others have sunk but not all the way. They are now just reefs, with only the tops of the volcanoes still visible. Others, like the active volcano Kilauea on the Big Island, remain high above the water. (The reason the Big Island has active volcanoes is because it is still over the hot spot.) The newest of the Hawaiian volcanoes—Loihi, which is located about 20 miles (30 km) southeast of the Big Island—has not yet reached the ocean's surface.

In Hawaii, four volcanoes have erupted in the past two hundred years. Today, thousands of people visit them. Three of the volcanoes—Mauna Loa, Kilauea, and Hualalai—are on the Big Island. Haleakala, which is in Haleakala National Park, is on Maui. Haleakala, which last erupted in 1801, is the world's largest dormant, or inactive, volcano. Mauna Loa, which last erupted in 1984, is the world's largest active volcano. Kilauea has erupted more than thirty times since 1952. The volcano Loihi, which is still underwater, keeps actively

## Hawaii Borders

Hawaii is surrounded in all directions by the Pacific Ocean.

# HAWAII
## COUNTY MAP

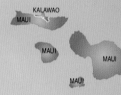

KAUAI

KAUAI

HONOLULU

KALAWAO

MAUI

MAUI

MAUI

MAUI

HAWAII

# HAWAII ★ ★ ★ ★ ★
## POPULATION BY COUNTY

| | |
|---|---:|
| Hawaii | 185,079 |
| Honolulu | 953,207 |
| Kalawao | 90 |
| Kauai | 67,091 |
| Maui | 154,834 |

Source: U.S. Bureau of the Census, 2010

**Olo'upena Falls drops 2,953 feet (900 m) on Molokai.**

**Leis are given as a sign of welcome to visitors to Hawaii.**

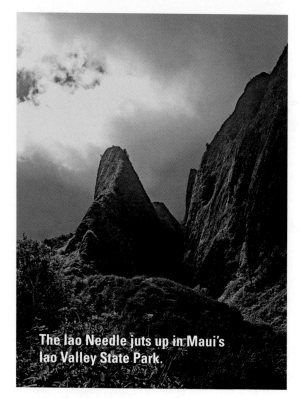
The Iao Needle juts up in Maui's Iao Valley State Park.

erupting. It could form a new island in ten thousand years.

Since 1983, there has been an area on Kilauea where the lava flow is active. In October 2014, it flowed into the town of Pahoa.

The forces of nature are strong in Hawaii. In addition to the volcanic eruptions, there have been earthquakes, hurricanes, and even tsunamis. A tsunami is a series of huge waves following an undersea disturbance such as an earthquake. Hilo was hit by tsunamis in 1946 and 1960.

## The Hawaiian Islands

Each of Hawaii's main islands is different. The island of Hawaii is the biggest—just over 4,000 square miles (10,400 sq km) in area—which is how it got its nickname of the Big Island. On the northern and southeastern coasts of the Big Island are high cliffs, with waterfalls that flow into the ocean. The Big Island has the second-largest population of any of the islands, with about 185,000 people.

Hawaii is a record holder among the states. Ka Lae, a point on the south side of the island of Hawaii, is the southernmost point in the United States. With its many islands and shoals, Hawaii is the widest state.

Maui, formed by two volcanoes, has many canyons on its mountainsides. There is an **isthmus** (a narrow strip of land that connects the two volcanoes) where the soil is rich and sugarcane grows easily. Maui is home to one of the world's largest banyan trees—it covers a city block—and home to the Iao Needle, a monolith (or mass of lava) that rises 1,200 feet (365 m) from the valley floor in Iao Valley State Park. Maui has a population of more than 154,000. Residents live in a few large towns and "upcountry," or out in a rural area where there are small villages.

The unpopulated island of Kahoolawe lies next to Maui. Until 1990, the US Navy tested bombs there. The bombing left the island barren and dry. Efforts are now under way to clean up the island and reintroduce native plants.

For hundreds of years, the small and relatively wild island of Molokai was populated. But in the 1860s, most of the healthy residents left after a leper colony was established there by the Hawaiian legislature and King Kamehameha V. **Leprosy**—now called Hansen's disease—is a contagious disease that causes serious skin lesions and damage to the nerves, muscles, and eyes. Today, the island is home to a population of around eight thousand people, including a small group that still lives in the former leper colony.

The small island of Lanai, which measures just 18 miles (30 km) in length and 13 miles (20 km) in width, was once covered almost entirely by pineapple plantations. Now, it is home to luxury resorts. Lanai has about three thousand residents.

Oahu is the most populated island. There are a few stretches of wild coastline left on the island, but in other places it is almost entirely filled with businesses and homes. Oahu is known for Waikiki Beach, a white-sand beach lined with resorts and hotels. The state's capital city of Honolulu, located on Oahu, has both beautiful tropical landscapes and modern high-rise buildings.

Kauai is known for its amazing Waimea Canyon. This canyon, lined with exotic vegetation, is 10 miles (16 km) long. The canyon was formed by rivers and floodwaters flowing down Mount Waialeale, which is one of the wettest places on Earth. The island has

**Waimea Canyon on Kauai was carved by a lot of rainwater.**

**Aloha Tower**

**Haleakala**

**Hawaii Volcanoes National Park**

## 1. Aloha Tower

This lighthouse located in Honolulu was built in 1926. For decades it was the tallest structure in Hawaii. It offers spectacular views of the city and the harbor from its top.

## 2. Barking Sands

This famous beach is located on Kauai. When it is dry, its sand makes a sound like a barking dog when a person walks on it. There is a Pacific missile range facility here as well as cottages.

## 3. Haleakala

This is one of the largest inactive volcanic craters in the world, measuring 25 miles (40 km) around and 3,000 feet (915 m) deep. It is located on Maui and is the island's highest point at 10,023 feet (3,055 m). You can go on a wilderness hike, and see exotic plants, waterfalls, streams, and rocky coastlines in the National Park.

## 4. Hawaii Volcanoes National Park

Hawaii Volcanoes National Park is one of Hawaii's two national parks, and it is located on the Big Island. Visitors can drive along the 11-mile (17.7 km) road that encircles the summit and pass through several different **ecosystems**.

## 5. Kalaupapa National Historic Site

This is the site of the famous leper colony on Molokai run by Father Damien, a Belgian missionary priest who arrived here in 1873 and died of the disease he dedicated his life to fighting in 1889.

# HAWAII ★ ★ ★ ★

### 6. Kapiolani Park

Built on an extinct volcano by King Kalakaua in the 1870s, this 500-acre (202-hectare) park on Oahu offers visitors the 42-acre (17 ha) Honolulu Zoo and a concert series. Many of the park's trees are more than one hundred years old. Also located here is Diamond Head, the famous volcanic tuff cone.

Kapiolani Park

### 7. Keahiakawelo

Also know as Garden of the Gods, this natural rock garden is located on Lanai. Its boulders and craggy rock towers were formed over centuries by erosion.

### 8. Menehune Fish Pond

This historic site was supposedly built a thousand years ago by Hawaii's first Polynesian settlers, the Menehune, a race of small people. Hawaiian royalty once ate the fish captured in the pond, formed by a dam across the Huleia River.

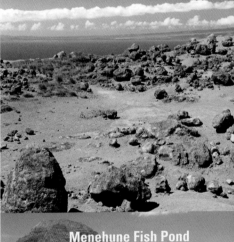
Keahiakawelo

### 9. Pearl Harbor Memorial

A natural harbor on Oahu, it was home to the US Pacific Fleet when it was attacked by Japanese planes on December 7, 1941. The centerpiece of this historic site is the battleship *Arizona*, which sunk that day. It lies on the harbor's bottom.

### 10. Polynesian Cultural Center

This living museum on Oahu is composed of eight Polynesian villages with residents from Hawaii, Fiji, New Zealand, Tonga, Samoa, Tahiti, Marquesas, and Aotearo. Visitors can see traditional dancing and entertainment, and enjoy a **luau**, a Hawaiian feast.

Menehune Fish Pond

a population of roughly sixty thousand people, who live mostly in the island's small towns located along the coasts.

Niihau is privately owned. Only the owners, their workers, and their guests see this island. Niihau has a population of 250 people, almost all of whom are of Polynesian descent.

## A Natural Paradise

Even though some cities are filled with modern buildings and crowds, the Hawaiian Islands still remain a place of astounding natural beauty. Surrounded by deep blue seas, the islands have beautiful beaches. In some places, the sand on these beaches is white and sparkling. Other beaches are made of black sand, formed when molten lava from a volcano poured into the ocean, cooled, and eventually wore down into sand particles. Other portions of Hawaii's coastlines offer dramatically high cliffs.

Hawaii's volcanic mountains all lie inland, and most of them are covered in thick tropical growth. Guava bushes, ferns, mango trees, and many more plants grow along the slopes.

Mauna Kea is the tallest mountain in the world. Measured from its base at the ocean floor to its tip, it has an elevation of about 18,000 feet (5,500 m) below sea level and another 13,796 feet (4,205 m) above sea level. The total elevation is well over 31,000 feet (9,450 m), much more than Asia's Mount Everest, which is about 29,000 feet (8,840 m).

Silversword grows on the dry side of Mauna Kea.

Mauna Loa and Mauna Kea are so high that they can be snow-covered in winter.

Hawaii is home to several spectacularly different and fragile ecosystems. Ecosystems are natural areas in which living organisms—plants and animals—interact. A rain forest is an example of an ecosystem. On Mauna Loa, there is a rain forest where the jungle is thick and full of birds. On one side of Mauna Kea, on the other hand, there is a different, dry forest. Little rain falls on the area, which is perfect for plants such as silversword—a rare, low-growing plant with clusters of pointed leaves and tall purple or red flowers—and for other desertlike plants, such as cacti.

The Hakalau Forest National Wildlife Refuge on the Big Island protects ohia and koa trees, which are large and can reach heights of up to 80 feet (24 m). Especially interesting is the terrain around Kilauea, where lava flows often destroy the plants. Despite this, tiny new plants manage to push up through the lava and grow. The Big Island is also home to the lush Waipio Valley.

Although there are no large rivers or lakes in Hawaii, there are many beautiful small rivers and estuaries, the aquatic habitats at the mouths of rivers. The Wailuku River, which starts on the slopes of Mauna Kea on the Big Island, is the state's longest river. Kauai has several rivers, too. They are popular with kayakers.

## In Their Own Words

"For me, the magic of Hawaii comes from the stillness, the sea, the stars."

—Author Joanne Harris

The useful koa tree can reach heights of 100 feet (30 m).

Hawaii is also the location of some of the world's most spectacular waterfalls. Olo'upena Falls on Molokai is the fourth-tallest waterfall in the world. Another interesting natural water phenomenon is the blowhole, where ocean water spouts up through lava tubes.

## Hawaii's Climate

Hawaii has only two true seasons: summer (called Kau in Hawaiian), which runs from May to October, and winter (called Hooilo), which runs from November to April. Although it can be humid in Hawaii, trade winds usually bring cool air off the ocean, and temperatures are consistent throughout the year. The average daytime summer temperature at sea level is 85 degrees Fahrenheit (29 degrees Celsius). The average daytime winter temperature is 78°F (25°C). The highest temperature ever recorded in Hawaii was 100°F (38°C). That record was set in 1931 at Pahala on the Big Island. Temperatures can be cold in the mountains.

Each island has a windward side and a leeward side. The windward side is reached first by the prevailing winds blowing in off the Pacific Ocean, and it tends to be cooler and to get more rain. The leeward side is more protected from the winds off the ocean water, and it tends to be sunnier, warmer, and drier.

Rainfall varies greatly over the islands. On the island of Hawaii, the small port of Kawaihae, located on the northwestern shore, typically gets only 8 or 9 inches (20 or 23 centimeters) of rain per year. But the city of Hilo, located on the eastern shore of the Big Island, gets an average of 130 inches (330 cm) per year. On Kauai, Mount Waialeale—one of the wettest places on Earth—averages more than 460 inches (1,170 cm) of rain per year.

## Hawaii's Plant Life

When many people think of trees in Hawaii, palm trees often come to mind. But Hawaii has many other kinds of trees. One of these is the ohia, a very tall tree covered with red, yellow, or orange lehua flowers, that grows on volcanic slopes. Another is the koa tree. The hard red wood of koa trees was used to make canoes in earlier times and is used to make furniture today.

Plants that Hawaiians grow for food include sugarcane, pineapple, papaya, banana, mango, guava, lichee, avocado, breadfruit, macadamia nut, lime, passion fruit, and tamarind. There are also many different flowers that bloom all over Hawaii. These include orchids, anthuriums, and plumeria.

## Animals in Hawaii

Before humans came, the hoary bat and the monk seal were the only mammals native to Hawaii. There were also many kinds of native lizards, insects, and birds. Offshore, a variety of fish, including marlin, dolphin, and tuna, swam in the waters. Today, hundreds of species of fish live in Hawaiian waters.

The seeds of some plants came to Hawaii by air, carried by birds or the wind. Other seeds came by water, drifting across the ocean. Since the islands were so isolated for so long, different species developed in new ways. Today, Hawaii has many plants and animals that are not found anywhere else.

The islands' first inhabitants brought with them dogs and pigs. They also brought rats, which had hidden in their boats and canoes. Later, Europeans brought cats, horses, cattle, goats, and sheep.

Because of loss of habitat, pollution, and other changes to the land and water, many species in the Hawaiian Islands are endangered, or in danger of completely dying out. Hawaiians are working to keep these species from disappearing forever.

Pygmy killer whales live miles off the coast of the Hawaiian Islands.

Green Sea Turtles

Hawaiian Monk Seal

Honeycreeper

## 1. Green Sea Turtle

When baby green sea turtles hatch, their shells are only about 2 inches (5 cm) long. Adult turtles may weigh more than 400 pounds (180 kg). Scientists believe green sea turtles can live eighty years or more.

## 2. Hawaiian Hoary Bat

Hawaiian hoary bats are forest dwellers that hunt over open land. Unlike most bats, which live in colonies, they roost or make their homes alone. These bats are endangered.

## 3. Hawaiian Monk Seal

Hawaiian monk seals are one of only two mammals native to Hawaii. Measuring up to 8 feet (2.4 m) in length and weighing up to 600 pounds (270 kg), monk seals dive up to 500 feet (150 m) below the ocean surface for prey.

## 4. Honeycreeper

Honeycreeper birds live in forests high on the mountains. The most interesting-looking honeycreepers are brightly colored and have curved bills. These bills help them drink nectar out of flowers. The 'I'iwi is a brilliant red honeycreeper with a hooked bill that lives in forests of ohia trees.

## 5. Humpback Whale

Adult humpback whales weigh about 79,000 pounds (36,000 kg) and live on a diet mostly of small fish and tiny sea creatures called krill. The males "sing" a song that lasts up to twenty minutes and can be repeated for hours.

## 6. Lokelani Rose

This bright flower is the official flower of Maui. It is a favorite of gardeners for its sweet fragrance and its beauty. It was first brought to the islands in the 1800s, possibly by New England sailors.

## 7. Nene

The black and white nene, or Hawaiian goose, was almost extinct by the 1940s. A special recovery program was set up during the 1970s. Today, there are approximately nine hundred nene in the wild and about two thousand in breeding programs and zoos.

## 8. Ohia Tree

Ohia trees produce an attractive red flower called the lehua. A Hawaiian myth says that the goddess Pele fell in love with the warrior Ohia, but he was already in love with a girl named Lehua. Pele was so angry that she turned him into a tree and Lehua became a flower.

## 9. Pineapple

Although long associated with Hawaii, the pineapple plant is native to southern Brazil and was brought to the Islands in the early 1800s. Pineapples contain a substance called bromelain that is used in medicines and meat tenderizer.

## 10. Triggerfish

Hawaiian waters—especially aound the coral reefs—are home to the triggerfish. Different types of triggerfish have distinctive markings. One type is the humuhumunukunukuapua'a, or humuhumu for short.

Lokelani Rose

Ohia Tree

Triggerfish

Traditional or voyaging canoes may have carried people from Tahiti to settle in Hawaii.

# From the Beginning

Hawaii was one of the last places on Earth to be settled by humans. Scientists believe Polynesians—people from islands in the central and southern Pacific Ocean—arrived in Hawaii sometime between 300 and 750 CE.

For years, Polynesians traveled to and from the different islands in the Pacific Ocean. To get to many of these islands, they built huge seagoing canoes. Each canoe was big enough to hold dozens of people and to travel thousands of miles. Because there were no maps and no landmarks in the middle of the ocean, travelers had to depend on natural signs to tell them where they were. These signs included ocean swells, currents, winds, and cloud formations. At night, they read the stars to find their way.

Experts believe that Polynesian travelers—probably from the Marquesas, which are islands in the southern Pacific Ocean—set out to find a new place to settle. These settlers might have been the first to arrive in the Hawaiian Islands. A second wave of settlement in Hawaii occurred around 1000 to 1300 CE. These new people probably came from Tahiti, an island in the South Pacific.

# Two Ideas

There has been some debate about the settlement of Hawaii. A Norwegian named Thor Heyerdahl believed Polynesians were descended from the people of Peru. In 1947, he set out on a raft made of balsa wood and made the voyage from Peru to Hawaii. He wanted to prove that people would drift on the tides from South America to the islands in the South Pacific. He believed those islands were settled by an accidental discovery.

He called his boat *Kon-Tiki* and designed it so it could have been made by ancient people. It took Heyerdahl and his crew three months to finish their voyage. He wrote a best-selling book about the trip. There was a movie was made about the voyage in 2012.

To counter the drift theory of settlement, another voyage was planned. A traditional navigator named Pius "Mau" Piailug guided the Hawaiian voyaging canoe *Hokule'a* on a 2,500-mile (4,023 km) trip from Hawaii to Tahiti. Piailug read the night sky and the swell of the oceans to guide his boat. He knew the rising and the setting of the sun could be used to know your direction during the day. These skills required a lot of knowledge about the change of the location of the stars at different latitudes. Piailug also knew that ocean swells changed when they bounced off of islands. So, he could feel the presence of land before it could be seen.

Outrigger canoes were used to make long ocean voyages.

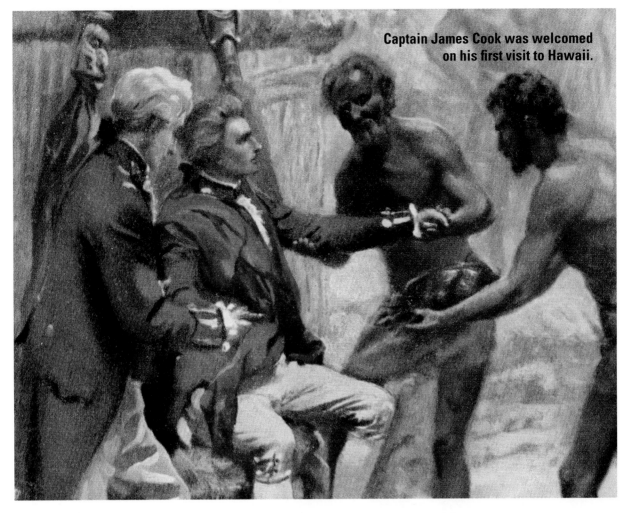

Captain James Cook was welcomed on his first visit to Hawaii.

His navigation methods proved that Polynesian navigators, despite not having a written language or instruments, were masters of the sea. This proved they were capable of settling Hawaii. The first Europeans to explore the area came upon further proof. They discovered that the languages of Hawaii and distant islands such as Tahiti were very similar. People from the islands could speak with each other.

Most of what is known of ancient Hawaiian history comes from stories told by the Hawaiian people. This form of storytelling is called oral tradition. Stories and myths have been passed down from one generation to the next. Archaeologists (scientists who study the artifacts, or remains, of ancient peoples) face challenges trying to add information because weather and time have destroyed most of the islands' ancient buildings and artifacts.

## Captain Cook

In 1778, the first European ships landed at Waimea on Kauai. British navy captain James Cook, one of the most important explorers of his day, was their commander. Hawaiian

# The Native People

The Hawaiian Islands were uninhabited until the arrival of Polynesians from the Marquesas Islands in the South Pacific between 300 and 500 CE. A second group of settlers arrived from Tahiti around 1200 CE. Historians do not agree about what happened between these groups—some say the Tahitians enslaved the first settlers. Eventually a single culture evolved despite land wars between ruling chieftains. There are not different tribes among the native population.

The Native Hawaiians built a society with many classes, with a king at the top and outcasts at the bottom. They developed surfing and the art of hula. They built temples to worship their gods and their ancestors, and they came up with new ways to make and color *kapa*, a cloth made from plant fibers. Trade was set up between people on the coasts and those in the mountains, and almost everything came from plant life.

Traditional Hawaiian statues carved out of wood are set at Pu'uhonua o Honaunau National Historical Park on the Big Island.

The Hawaiians had no metal tools or pottery. They made tools out of stone or bone, and made bowls and containers out of gourds, or by carving or weaving them.

There were 400,000 to 800,000 Native Hawaiians when British Captain James Cook arrived in the region in 1778. Protestant missionaries arrived in 1820, along with fishermen and whalers. Disease came with them, and it killed 80 to 90 percent of the Native population. A French ship that came to the island in 1780 found the majority of the islanders ill. By 1832, their numbers dropped to 130,000. By 1919, there were only 22,600 native Hawaiians left.

The Hawaiians integrated much better with the non-native

population compared to Native Americans in the continental United States. Hawaiians have intermarried with other ethnic groups, such as Asians and Latinos. The US Census Bureau recognizes Native Hawaiian and Other Pacific Islander as a race. This group makes up 10 percent of Hawaii's population. People identifying themselves as Native Hawaiian make up 5.9 percent of the state's population.

## The Native Hawaiians

The word "Hawaii" may have come from Hawaiki, a native word for "homeland."

**Social Structure:** The kings, chiefs, and priests ruled each individual Hawaiian island, but the islands were not united into a single kingdom. Chiefs claimed large plots of land as well as areas along the coast. They gave smaller portions of land to the rest of the people to farm. Most people had to grow enough food to give an annual tribute to their chief as well as feed their families.

**Religion:** Ancient Hawaiians worshiped Ku, the god of war. Many of the Hawaiians' other gods were of nature. Children grew up hearing legends of Pele, the goddess of volcanoes, whom Hawaiians believed demanded human sacrifice. Public worship took place in a temple called a *heiau*. Inside the heiau there was an altar, a raised platform, and carved images.

**Food:** The diet of the Hawaiians was rich in seafood, including squid, octopus, and many kinds of fish. They pounded the taro root into a food called poi, a rich carbohydrate that remains a staple of the Hawaiian diet to this day. Their meats came from pigs, chickens, and a variety of birds that they hunted. Other foods included yams, seaweed, fan palm, and tree fern.

**Clothing:** Hawaiians wore light clothing suitable for their warm climate. The men wore a loincloth called a malo, and the women wore a skirt called a *pai'u*. Both were fashioned from kapa, a barkcloth made from plant fibers.

**Art:** The arts were important to the ancient Hawaiians. They used wood, shell, stone, and bone in carvings and jewelry. They developed elaborate calendars that told them when to plant certain crops.

**Recreation:** Athletic contests in events such as canoe racing and swimming were frequently held. Ancient Hawaiians traveled by canoe to fish and to visit other islands, sometimes to trade and other times to fight.

myth explained that one day the god Lono would come from the sea on a floating island. Many Hawaiians believed that Cook was this god.

Captain Cook judged his first visit to Hawaii as a great success. His crews greatly enjoyed the time they spent on the islands. He described them as a tropical paradise.

## Naming the Islands

Captain Cook initially called Hawaii the Sandwich Islands after his patron, the English Earl of Sandwich. King Kamehameha renamed them the Kingdom of Hawaii in 1819.

When he returned in 1779 for a second visit, however, trouble erupted. Cook and a few natives on the Big Island got into an argument over a boat that the British believed the natives had stolen. Cook was killed and his crew fled the islands on their ships.

Cook's death did not end European interest in the islands. The British wanted to establish trade with China. One thing the Chinese wanted was sandalwood, which grew in Hawaii. European and American traders came to Hawaii to look for the sweet-smelling sandalwood to sell in China for a great deal of money.

## A New Kingdom

Around the time Captain Cook first visited the islands, a young warrior named Kamehameha lived in Kohala on the northern shores of the Big Island. He fought to rule the island, and by 1790, he controlled most of it. From there, he fought for control of the other islands. By 1810, having united all the islands into a single kingdom, he had become Hawaii's first king.

Kamehameha I welcomed people from other countries. He found them interesting and liked the goods they brought. Over time, Hawaiians became more and more accustomed to the foreigners. A few Hawaiians even agreed to leave Hawaii to travel to other lands. In Great Britain and the United States, these Hawaiians created a great stir. **Missionaries**—people who traveled to new places to spread their religion—were interested in bringing their Christian beliefs to the islands and the people who lived there.

In 1819, two important things happened. First, King Kamehameha I died. He was succeeded by his son, Kamehameha II, who was advised by one of the late king's wives. Second, American whaling ships came for the first time. With the arrival of the whalers, Hawaii's ports began to develop. The whaling ships returned to Hawaii every winter.

A statue of Kamehameha I, who united Hawaii into a kingdom, stands outside a building that houses the state Supreme Court.

# Making a Hawaiian Lei

**Leis** are popular gifts for visitors to Hawaii. Leis are garlands or wreaths made of fresh flowers, but you can make your own using construction paper.

## What You Need

Sheets of colored construction paper

A pen or pencil

Scissors

Hole puncher

A shoelace

Colored straws

## What to Do

- Draw flower shapes on the construction paper with a pen or pencil. Use the scissors to cut out the flower shapes.
- Using the hole puncher, punch a hole in the center of the flowers.
- Cut the straws into inch-long (2.5 cm long) pieces.
- Thread the flower shapes and pieces of straw onto the shoelace, alternating flower, straw, flower, straw.
- Tie the ends of the shoelace together.
- Give your Hawaiian lei to a friend or wear it yourself.

Christian missionaries reached the Hawaiian Islands in 1820.

## Surfing Royalty

The ancient Polynesians of Hawaii invented surfing, which they called *he'enalu*. It originally was part of their religion and was practiced only by royalty. Hawaiian princes and kings surfed on 20-foot [6 m] boards that weighed more than 150 pounds [68 kilograms].

In 1820, after voyages that lasted many months, missionaries arrived from New England. Over the years, fifteen different groups of missionaries came. The missionaries affected the lives of Hawaiian people in many ways. For instance, the missionaries forced Hawaiians to stop wearing their traditional clothing and dancing the hula. The missionaries also developed a written Hawaiian language and taught many native people to read and write. This written Hawaiian alphabet contains only twelve letters: the vowels *a, e, i, o,* and *u* and the consonants *h, k, l, m, n, p,* and *w.* Two symbols— the okina (the ' mark) and the macron (a line placed over a letter)—are also parts of the alphabet. The okina signifies a pause between syllables. The missionaries brought European and American education to Hawaii. Maui's Lahainaluna is the oldest high school west of the Rockies. It was founded by missionaries in 1831.

## Life Among Exiles

One missionary whose name is associated with Hawaii did a great deal of good for unfortunate people who were being discriminated against. His name is Father Damien, and he was named a saint in the Catholic Church in 2009.

In the mid-1800s, the disease then called leprosy was brought to Hawaii from China. It became an epidemic. In 1865, the legislature passed the Act to Prevent the Spread of Leprosy and King Kamehameha V ordered that anyone who has this incurable disease should be separated from the population. People were afraid of leprosy because no one knew how it was spread. Victims were sent to an area on the island of Molokai called Kalawao. It was surrounded on three sides by ocean and by high cliffs on the other. This prevented the people put there from reaching other parts of the island.

The only way to get to Kalawao was by boat. The first group left Honolulu in 1866. Sometimes, crewmembers on the boats carrying victims of the disease were very afraid of

Victims of Hansen's disease (leprosy) were isolated in a small settlement on the island of Molokai.

becoming ill. Instead of taking those people all the way to Kalawao, they forced them to swim to the shore.

In 1873, Armauer Hansen discovered that a bacteria, called *Mycobacterium leprae*, caused the disease. Infection was caused by repeated contact with this bacteria. That is why the illness is called Hansen's disease. Father Damien arrived in Hawaii in 1864 and was sent to Kalawao in 1873, one year after the first church was set up there.

Father Damien, born Joseph De Veuster in Belgium in 1840, changed life in Kalawao. Conditions there were horrible. He helped build homes, established a water system, set up schools, and cared for the sick. He asked the government of Hawaii for more assistance. There were many other religious people helping the ill on Molokai, but Father Damien drew the interest of people around the world.

## Holiday for a King

Hawaii is the only state to honor a monarch with a holiday. King Kamehameha Day was first celebrated on June 11, 1872, the year of Kamehameha V's death.

Father Damien lived among those with Hansen's disease, eating with them and changing their bandages. He did not protect himself with proper hygiene. He contracted the disease and died April 15, 1889. Others came to the island to continue his work. Among those who did was Mother Marianne Cope, who was nicknamed Mother Marianne of Molokai. She was raised in Utica, New York, and in 2012 also was named a saint by the Catholic Church.

There were about eight thousand people exiled to Molokai. That practice ended when the law separating people suffering from Hansen's disease from their families was repealed in 1969. Patients are still treated in the hospital on Molokai. The Kalaupapa National Historical Park, named for the peninsula on which Kalawao was located, was established in 1980.

## Ruling Family

Kamehameha's family remained in power for five generations. Under the influence of the missionaries, Kamehameha III developed a written constitution in 1840. He also passed the Great Mahele in 1848, which established a system of land ownership, letting people other than the king—including foreigners—own property.

Kamehameha III and his successor, Kamehameha IV, faced challenges from Europeans and Americans, however. For a long time, Great Britain, France, and the United States had all promised to allow Hawaii to remain independent. But all of these countries wanted

# 10 KEY CITIES

Hilo

Kailua

## 1. Honolulu: population 371,657

Honolulu, the capital of Hawaii, is located on the island of Oahu. It is a vibrant cultural center, the gateway to the islands, an important hub for international business, and a major tourist destination. It is home to the fourth-largest marathon in the US.

## 2. Pearl City: population 47,698

Pearl City is located along the north shore of Pearl Harbor, Oahu. It covers only 5 square miles (13 sq km). In 2007, a Pearl City baseball team, Pearl City Little League, won the Junior League World Series for players ages 13–14.

## 3. Hilo: population 43,698

Hilo is the largest city on the Big Island and home to the University of Hawaii at Hilo, the Imiloa Astronomy Center of Hawaii, and the Mauna Loa Macadamia Nut Corporation. It sits on Hilo Bay, surrounded by two volcanoes. One of them, Mauna Loa, is an active volcano.

## 4. Kailua: population 38,635

Kailua is a largely residential city in Honolulu County. *Kailua* means "two seas" in Hawaiian, referring to the two lagoons that run through nearby Kailua Bay. Kailua Beach has often been called Hawaii's best beach.

## 5. Waipahu: population 38,216

Waipahu is a former sugar plantation town on Oahu. One of its highlights is the Hawaiian Plantation Village, an outdoor museum dedicated to interpreting the experiences of plantation workers.

# HAWAII ★ ★ ★ ★

### 6. Kane'ohe: population 34,597

Kane'ohe is a residential city in the county of Honolulu. *Kane'ohe* in Hawaiian means "bamboo man." It got its name from an old legend about a local woman who said her husband's cruelty was like the sharp edge of cutting bamboo. A landmark is the Ho'omaluhia Botanical Garden with its exotic plants and flowers.

### 7. Mililani Town: population 27,629

Mililani Town is located in the center of Oahu and is mostly a residential community. Formerly the location of plantation fields, Mililani was named an All-America City in 1986, the only city in Hawaii to be so honored.

### 8. Kahului: population 26,337

Kahului is located on Maui and serves as the island's shopping hub. It is also home to a sugar museum, the Kanaha Pond State Wildlife Sanctuary, and the Maui Arts and Cultural Center.

### 9. 'Ewa Gentry: population 22,690

'Ewa Gentry is a residential community about 12 miles (19 km) from Oahu. More than a century ago, 'Ewa was one of the biggest cities in Hawaii and a center of the sugar cane industry. *'Ewa* in Hawaiian means "crooked."

### 10. Kihei: population 20,881

Kihei is in central Maui. It is home to the main offices of the Hawaiian Islands Humpback Whale National Marine Sanctuary and the Maui Research and Technology Park, where the Maui High Performance Computing Center (MHPCC) is located.

Kane'ohe

Kihei

to possess the islands, especially after Hawaii became a major producer and exporter of sugarcane. Many of the sugarcane plantations were owned by foreigners (often former missionary families), and as the years went on, cheap labor was brought in from other countries, such as China and Japan.

In 1872, Kamehameha V died. In the years that followed, there were struggles over the throne. In addition, US influence became greater and greater. This was especially true after people such as Honolulu-born Sanford Dole established pineapple plantations on the islands. The business owners, including people from the United States, wanted a great deal of say in how the islands were run.

## Hawaii and the United States

In 1875, Hawaii and the United States signed a reciprocity treaty. Planters and other business owners wanted to have this special kind of treaty, which set out rules for trading and selling Hawaiian goods. The US government said that Hawaii could sell sugar and

Power was taken from Queen Liliuokalani when Hawaii was annexed by the United States.

other Hawaiian products in the United States without having to pay an extra tax. Eventually, the United States was granted permission to build a naval base at Hawaii's Pearl Harbor, on Oahu.

The reciprocity treaty gave those who owned businesses what they wanted, but only for a time. A change came in 1890, when the US Congress passed the McKinley Tariff, which increased taxes on foreign sugar. With sugar from Hawaii now more expensive in the US than sugar grown in Florida and other states, Hawaiian sugar planters suffered. The islands fell into an economic depression. The only way to avoid the tax was to become part of the United States. When efforts began to restore some of the power of the monarchy, the businessmen soon started to talk about **annexation**, which meant adding Hawaii to the United States.

Native Hawaiians did not want their land to become part of the United States. They preferred to remain free and independent. In 1893, after Hawaiian queen Liliuokalani introduced a new constitution, Americans living in Hawaii—led by Sanford Dole and acting on their own—overthrew her kingdom. They were helped by US Marines. They took away her power and started their own government in Hawaii.

United States president Grover Cleveland demanded that Hawaii be given back to its people. He withdrew an annexation treaty from the Senate and ordered an investigation into the incident. He wanted to restore the queen to her throne. Those who had taken over Hawaii ignored Cleveland's wishes and formed a republic in 1894, with Dole as president.

In 1898, during the four months of the Spanish American War, the United States needed the military bases on Hawaii for their fight against the Spanish in the Philippines. Leaders in the United States had come to consider Hawaii a necessity for defending the Pacific region, so under the presidency of William McKinley, the Hawaiian Islands were annexed by the United States. Many native Hawaiians remained opposed, but the United States was too powerful. In 1900, the Hawaiian Islands were formally organized as a US territory, with Sanford Dole as governor. (Throughout the history of the United States, new lands were often organized as territories before becoming states.)

## Deadliest Eruption

An eruption of the volcano Kilauea on the Big Island in 1790 killed more than five thousand people and remains the most deadly volcanic eruption ever in what is now the United States.

James Dole (a distant cousin of Sanford Dole) arrived from Massachusetts in 1899 and became a major figure for Hawaii. Pineapple is not native to Hawaii. It is believed to have originated in South America, near the border of Brazil, Paraguay, and Argentina. Spanish sailor Don Francisco de Paula Marin is often given credit for bringing the fruit to the islands in the 1790s. Before the invention of ways to keep fruit fresh in cans, it was impossible to get pineapple from Hawaii to the United States before it went bad. James Dole opened the Hawaiian Pineapple Company in 1901. He had machines built that could peel and process one hundred pineapples each minute. He joined with other growers to do promotional work that made people connect Hawaii with pineapples. Recipes such as pineapple upside-down cake made the fruit a fad item, so processing it was a successful business for decades.

Miss Bryan.   General John C. Black.   Fred. W. Job,   Major Iauken,   Judge Grosscup.   Thomas W. Cridler,   Charles Page Bryan,   Mrs. Brooke.   Major-General Brooke.   Hon. Francis M. Hatch,
Hawaiian Consul.   A.D.C. to Pres. of Hawaii.   Third Ass.. Sec'y of State.   Minister to Brazil.   Minister of Hawaii.

Sanford Dole, seated in the middle of the front row, became president of the republic of Hawaii in 1894.

Hon. Thomas B. Bryan, Pres. Union League Club.   Mrs. John C. Black.   Mrs. Thomas B. Bryan.   Com'r. Phelps, U.S.N.   President Dole.   Major Heistand, U.S.A.   Mrs. Dole.   Mrs Grosscup.

# The Twentieth Century

In the opening decades of the twentieth century, Hawaiians began to realize they could make money and help their economy by attracting tourists to the islands. A tourist committee was formed for the first time in 1903. In 1915, *The Aloha Guide*—the first guidebook devoted to Hawaii—was published. The first luxury passenger ship docked in Hawaii in 1927.

During the early years of the twentieth century, the islands attracted both tourists and new residents, and Hawaii's population grew rapidly. In 1900, the territory had a population of 154,001. By 1920, the number climbed to 255,881. In 1935, planes first carried mail across the Pacific, from California to the Philippines, with stops in Hawaii and other Pacific islands.

## In Their Own Words

"We need Hawaii just as much and a good deal more than we did California. It is Manifest Destiny."

—President William McKinley

Growth of tourism was accompanied by the development of military bases in Hawaii. It is one of the only places in the middle of the Pacific Ocean where ships can safely dock for long periods of time. Its location is strategic. In the early 1900s, the US Navy built an important naval base at Pearl Harbor, a sheltered bay on Oahu.

Pearl Harbor later played a meaningful role in World War II, which began in Europe in 1939. On December 7, 1941, Japanese bombers taking off from aircraft carriers attacked US naval ships and planes located at Pearl Harbor and nearby air bases, killing some 2,400 Americans. Eighteen American ships and nearly three hundred airplanes were crippled or destroyed in the attack. The surprise attack forced the United States to enter World War II.

During the war, Japan was the enemy of the United States. Life became difficult for Japanese immigrants and Japanese Americans living on the US mainland and in Hawaii. Even though most of them did not support Japan, they suffered from discrimination and poor treatment. Internment camps were built and many people of Japanese descent were forced to live in them. There were at least five camps in Hawaii. There were far fewer

**The USS *Arizona* burns in Pearl Harbor on December 7, 1941.**

people of Japanese heritage forced to live in camps in Hawaii than on the US mainland, although some of those people were sent to camps on the mainland. Many of them were fired from their jobs or forced out of business. World War II ended in 1945, but years passed before Japanese Americans were treated as equal members of society.

## Hawaiian Statehood

After the war was over, Hawaii headed toward statehood. In March 1959, the US Congress passed an act making Hawaii a state, which President Dwight D. Eisenhower signed into law. Then, in June, Hawaiians voted on whether they wanted to become a state or not. They voted overwhelmingly in favor of statehood, 94 percent to 6 percent.

Finally, on August 21, 1959, Hawaii officially became the fiftieth US state. Alaska had become the forty-ninth state just eight months earlier. On this occasion, President Dwight Eisenhower said, "We will wish for [Hawaii] prosperity, security, happiness and a growing, closer relationship with all of the other states. We know that she is ready to do her part to make this Union a stronger nation." Many Hawaiians celebrated the occasion. They would now receive full representation in the federal government. Their voices would

A memorial rests above the USS *Arizona*, allowing visitors to view the sunken battleship and read the names of the sailors who died on it.

There are groups of native Hawaiians who want independence and a return to the constitution that existed under Queen Liliuokalani.

be heard, and they would receive the same benefits from the US government that people in all states receive.

## Favorite of Filmmakers

Hawaii has been the location for hundreds of feature films, from silent movies to today. It has also been the site for at least twenty-three television series, including two versions of *Hawaii Five-O, Fantasy Island,* and *Magnum, P.I.*

In the 1960s and the following decades, Hawaii saw changes as tourism became the state's major industry. Things changed again, however, when Asia's economy became troubled in 1995 and the numbers of visitors from that part of the world decreased. Tourism fell off even more sharply after the terrorist attacks of September 11, 2001, because many travelers preferred not to fly. When people began to travel again in greater numbers, tourists returned to Hawaii. A record number of visitors, more than eight million, came in 2013.

Among the main tourist draws are the country's active volcanoes. Some of these volcanoes deposit lava right into the ocean, but some ooze lava that threatens towns. In June of 2014, a lava flow started from the continuously erupting Kilauea volcano. By November it had approached Pahoa town. It burned a rural house in October and got within 500 yards (457 m) of the main road. There are not a lot of people living in the region.

In recent years, a native Hawaiian independence movement has become active. Different groups believe that the islands were illegally seized in 1893, when Queen Liliuokalani and her monarchy were overthrown. In 1993, the US Congress passed a resolution called the Apology Bill apologizing to native Hawaiians for the overthrow and the participation of US citizens and "agents."

The Office of Hawaiian Affairs, a state agency, has been charged with representing the interests of native Hawaiians since 1978. In addition, the US Congress continues to consider a bill to give federal recognition to the special status of native Hawaiians. Former Senator Daniel Akaka proposed a bill in Congress to recognize the native Hawaiians as an Indian tribe empowered to meet with the US government. Some natives do not want Hawaiians divided by race because it could split them on the question of self-determination. They want all Hawaiians to vote on whether the Islands should again become their own nation with its original constitution, as they were before 1893.

In 2008, Barack Obama was elected president of the United States. He became the country's first African-American president and the first president from Hawaii. Obama was born in Honolulu on August 4, 1961. He was raised in Oahu until age six and then returned with his mother at age ten when he attended the prestigious Punahou School. He later played basketball on the state championship team. Obama left the islands to attend Columbia University, but returned regularly to visit with family. As president, Obama has spent several Christmas vacations in his native state and named one of his daughters Malia, a common Hawaiian name.

# 10 KEY DATES IN STATE HISTORY

**1. 300-750 CE**

The first Polynesians arrive in Hawaii, probably in dugout canoes from the Marquesas Islands. The distance from the Marquesas to Hawaii is 2,000 miles (3,217 km).

**2. February 14, 1779**

Captain James Cook is killed by natives during a second visit to what he calls the Sandwich Islands. His first visit with the ships HMS *Resolution* and *Discovery* was made in January 1778.

**3. 1810**

King Kamehameha I unifies the islands under his kingdom, first established in 1795.

**4. March 30, 1820**

Fourteen American Protestant missionaries arrive in Hawaii to convert the native people to Christianity and educate them.

**5. January 17, 1893**

Queen Liliuokalani, the last monarch of the Kingdom of Hawaii, is overthrown by nine Americans and four Europeans living in Hawaii. The following year they help islanders establish the Republic of Hawaii.

**6. July 12, 1898**

A joint resolution is passed by the US Congress that annexes Hawaii. Two years later it is organized as an official US territory.

**7. December 7, 1941**

Japanese warplanes attack the US Pacific Fleet at Pearl Harbor in Oahu, bringing the United States into World War II.

**8. August 21, 1959**

Hawaii becomes the fiftieth state eight months after Alaska became the forty-ninth state. Hawaiians become full United States citizens.

**9. December 3, 2002**

Republican Linda Lingle takes office as Hawaii's first female governor, serving from 2002 to 2010. She was also Hawaii's first Jewish governor.

**10. November 4, 2008**

Barack Obama is elected president of the United States, defeating Arizona Senator John McCain. He becomes the country's first African-American president and the first president born in Hawaii. Obama was elected to a second term in 2012.

Surfing is a popular pastime in Hawaii, but it once was the sport of kings.

# The People

Based on its population, Hawaii is ranked fortieth among the fifty states. According to the 2010 US Census, there were 1,360,301 people living in Hawaii as of April 1 of that year. Most Hawaiians—more than 950,000—live in Honolulu County.

## People from Many Lands

Before Captain Cook came to the islands in 1778, the only people who lived in Hawaii were of Polynesian descent. After Cook was killed the following year and traders started to visit, a few Europeans came to live on the islands.

In the late 1780s, trading ships sailed to Hawaii with crews that included many Chinese sailors. Some of them jumped ship, preferring to live in what looked like paradise than on the seas. More and more Chinese people came over the years, especially between 1850 and 1898.

The first US missionaries arrived in 1820. In the years that followed, the population of Americans living in Hawaii grew steadily. In addition to missionaries, businesspeople, merchants, and craftspeople came to the islands.

In the mid-1800s, people from the mainland United States acquired land in Hawaii and developed sugarcane and pineapple plantations. Large numbers of Asians, including

Chinese, Japanese, and Filipinos (people from the Philippines), came to work in the fields. Life for these workers and their families was extremely hard. Many worked for cruel bosses for almost no money. Nevertheless, many of these people remained in Hawaii. Some men sent for their relatives, while others married Hawaiian women.

## A Different Type of State

Today, Hawaii differs from the other forty-nine states because there is no ethnic majority. In other words, no single ethnic group makes up more than half of the population.

The largest group is of Asian descent. Asian Americans make up more than 38 percent of the population. Caucasians—or white people—make up almost one-quarter of the population. Native Hawaiians and people from other Pacific islands make up 10 percent of the population. The Hispanic population now also makes up almost 9 percent of the people of Hawaii. Many Hispanic people living in Hawaii came to the state from Puerto Rico or are of Puerto Rican descent. Only 1.6 percent of the people who live in Hawaii are African American. Less than 1 percent (0.3 percent) is Native American. With all of this diversity, it is no surprise that many Hawaiians are of mixed heritage. More than 23 percent of Hawaiians are descended from two or more races.

Many Hawaiian residents are from other states. Some Americans come to enjoy the tropical weather all year long. Others move to Hawaii to retire or start island-related businesses.

### One Word, Many Meanings

"Aloha" has traditionally meant affection, peace, compassion, and mercy in the Hawaiian language. Only since the nineteenth century has it come to be used as an English greeting to say goodbye and hello.

## Culture and Traditions

One especially interesting thing about visiting Hawaii is seeing the many Polynesian influences. Although not many native Hawaiians—people who are directly descended from the first residents—are left in the area, many of their ways, and other island traditions, remain alive. For example, it is customary in Hawaii to remove your shoes when you enter someone's house. Another custom is giving strings of flowers called leis to people to welcome them to Hawaii or to recognize a birthday or other special occasion.

The first cowboys in Hawaii were imported from Mexico by King Kamehameha III to handle wild cattle.

Many people on the islands like to wear loose-fitting, brightly colored clothing. Hawaiian shirts (also called aloha shirts), which are usually brightly colored and decorated with bright designs, are popular. Women also occasionally wear muumuus, which are long dresses decorated with flowers or patterns. During festivals and other celebrations, many Hawaiian women wear traditional clothing, such as grass skirts.

Then there are the Hawaiian cowboys who dress like American cowboys. Their history goes as far back as the 1790s, when British explorer George Vancouver brought a small herd of eight cattle to the islands. Eventually, the herd grew into large numbers of wild cattle, and King Kamehameha III hired three Mexican cowboys to handle the animals. There are now cowboys and ranches across the main islands. In fact, one of the biggest cattle ranches in the United States, called Parker Ranch, can be found on the Big Island.

The diet of Hawaiian residents resembles the diet of other Americans in many ways. But Hawaiians tend to eat more fruit because it is so plentiful on the islands. Many of the state's residents also eat traditional food such as poi. Poi is a dish made from the cooked and pounded root of the taro plant, which grows on the islands. To celebrate birthdays and other special occasions, many people in Hawaii hold feasts called luaus, which often feature a roasted pig.

# 10 KEY PEOPLE

Bethany Hamilton

Jack Johnson

Nicole Kidman

### 1. Father Damien

Born in 1840 in Belgium, Joseph de Veuster adopted the name Father Damien when he became a priest in the 1860s. In 1873, Father Damien went to Molokai to minister to the lepers who had been sent there to live.

### 2. Bethany Hamilton

This surfer from Kauai lost her left arm to a shark attack in 2003, when she was thirteen. She turned pro in 2007 and won the Surf N Sea Pipeline Women's Pro in 2014. She has appeared on the television show *The Amazing Race* with her husband, Adam Dirks.

### 3. Laird Hamilton

Laird Hamilton was born Laird Zerfas in San Francisco, California, in 1964. He moved soon after to Hawaii with his mother. He is called the greatest "big wave" surfer in the world, riding waves as high as 70 feet (20 m).

### 4. Jack Johnson

The singer/songwriter was born in Oahu in 1975, and he still lives there. Jack Johnson was the youngest person, at seventeen, to reach the finals of the Pipeline Masters surfing competition in Maui. After a surfing accident, he turned to music and has sold millions of recordings.

### 5. Nicole Kidman

The actress was born in Hawaii but moved with her family to Australia. Her many films include *The Hours*, for which she won an Academy Award for Best Actress.

## 6. Queen Liliuokalani

Hawaii's last monarch was born in Honolulu in 1838. She became queen after the death of her brother, King David Kalakaua, in 1891. Two years later, Americans living in Hawaii overthrew her kingdom. She was an accomplished songwriter, author, and defender of Hawaiian traditions.

## 7. Lois Lowry

A leading children's author known for writing about controversial subjects, Lois Lowry won the Newbery Award for her novels *Number the Stars* and *The Giver*, which was made into a movie.

## 8. Bruno Mars

This best-selling R&B singer moved to Los Angeles from Hawaii. His second album *Unorthodox Jukebox* rose to number one on the record charts. His number one songs include "Just the Way You Are" and "Grenade."

## 9. Bette Midler

This actress and singer was born and raised in Honolulu. While enrolled at the University of Hawaii, she landed a small movie role and then moved to Los Angeles. She has had hit records and many leading roles in movies.

## 10. Michelle Wie

Born in Honolulu in 1989 to Korean-born parents, Michelle Wie began playing golf at the age of four. By ten, she was the youngest person ever to qualify for a United States Golf Association (USGA) amateur championship. The Stanford University graduate won the US Womens Open in 2014.

Queen Liliuokalani

Bruno Mars

Michelle Wie

# Who Hawaiians Are

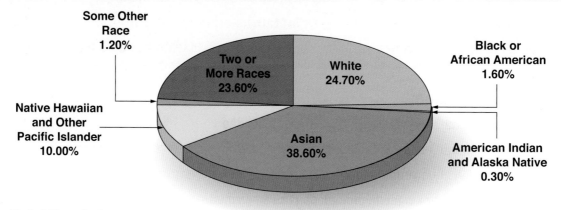

Some Other Race 1.20%

Two or More Races 23.60%

White 24.70%

Black or African American 1.60%

Native Hawaiian and Other Pacific Islander 10.00%

Asian 38.60%

American Indian and Alaska Native 0.30%

**Total Population**
**1,360,301**

Hispanic or Latino (of any race):
- 120,842 people (8.9%)

**Note:** The pie chart shows the racial breakdown of the state's population based on the categories used by the U.S. Bureau of the Census. The Census Bureau reports information for Hispanics or Latinos separately, since they may be of any race. Percentages in the pie chart may not add to 100 because of rounding.

Source: US Bureau of the Census, 2010 Census

Hawaiian culture remains in a state without a majority ethnic group.

Other elements of traditional Hawaiian culture include music and dance. Hawaiian music features instruments such as the ukulele and the slack-key guitar, which is tuned to produce unique sounds. There are also different types of drums made of gourds, sharkskin, coconuts, and other natural materials. As for dance, hula performances entertain residents and visitors and also honor the state's native history. Hawaiian Angela Perez Baraquio, who is of Filipino descent, wowed millions of television viewers when she danced the hula during the talent portion of the Miss America competition in 2001. She went on to win the crown.

The Hawaiian language is also still alive, although only about two thousand people speak the language fluently. However, those people who do not speak Hawaiian still know many words in the language. Many people use the word aloha as a greeting and call tourists malihini, a word that means "newcomer." Other Hawaiian words are *kai* (the sea), *mahalo* (thank you), *mauna* (mountain), and *ohana* (family). Interest in the language has grown in recent decades. The University of Hawaii has a Hawaiian language graduate studies program. Hawaiian place and street names have been added by the local government to new development projects. Students can attend so-called immersion schools where all subjects are taught in Hawaiian.

Pidgin is a type of slang language used in Hawaii. It is a mixture of English, Hawaiian, and Asian words. Pidgin was originally created so that immigrants from different countries could do business with native Hawaiians and Americans.

# Religion

The Catholic Church is the largest religious denomination in Hawaii, with about 350,000 followers. Catholic priests arrived in Honolulu on July 9, 1827, seven years after the first Protestant missionaries arrived. When the priests converted some of the natives to Catholicism, those natives were persecuted under order of the king and some chiefs and the priests were banished. Some of the native Catholics were jailed. On July 9, 1839, French forces on the frigate *Artémise* threatened to attack Honolulu unless the Catholics were let out of prison, that the Catholic religion was declared free, and that a site be found for a Catholic church. The king accepted these terms and the incident ended peacefully.

The Catholic Church is followed in number of practitioners by the Church of Jesus Christ of Latter-day Saints (Mormonism) and non-denominational Christian churches. After Christianity, the most popular religion is Buddhism, which about 9 percent of the population practices. Judaism is next with about ten thousand adherents. About half of all Hawaiians do not belong to any organized religion. The ancient Hawaiian practice of *Hoʻoponopono* is more a philosophy and way of life than a religion, but it has its own priests. They are called *kahuna lapaʻau* and are said to have healing powers. They preach forgiveness and emphasize the importance of prayer.

# Asian Influence

Hawaii is home to many people of Asian descent. Asian immigrants brought their customs, languages, and religions to Hawaii. In Honolulu, there is a large Chinatown. The area has never been limited to Chinese people, however. Chinese, Vietnamese, Laotian, Japanese, Thai, Filipino, and Korean people all have shops and restaurants there. People come to the markets to buy special Asian products and foods. These specialty items

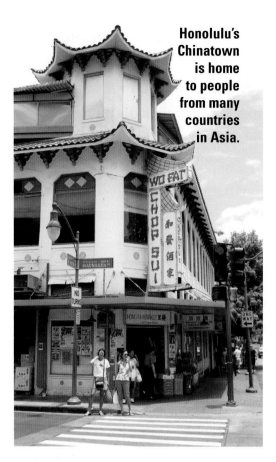

Honolulu's Chinatown is home to people from many countries in Asia.

include rice noodles and duck eggs. One of Hawaii's most popular spectator sports is sumo wrestling, which originated in Japan. Hawaii has more sumo wrestlers than any other state. A Hawaiian, Chad Rowan, was the first non-Japanese sumo wrestler to advance to yokozuna (Grand Champion) rank, the highest achievement in sumo wrestling.

Since the late twentieth century, historians have been collecting information about the history of Asian people in Hawaii. They have been trying to document, for example, the hard life that many Asian workers led on the islands' pineapple and sugarcane plantations.

Oral history projects collect people's stories, such as that of Japanese-born Tsuru Yamauchi, who moved to Hawaii in 1910 when she was twenty to join her husband, who already worked on a plantation. She explained her work on the plantation to an interviewer: "We moved to Number 10 Camp. I cooked and washed clothes there … At that time we had to wash everything by hand, scoop and carry the water from the faucet to the bathhouse … Oh, I sure did everything. And as for ironing, it was charcoal iron. We put in two pieces of charcoal and adjusted the heat until it got warm. I got paid one dollar a month per person. I did cooking, washing, everything. I got only one dollar. That is all."

A Japanese folk song, called a *hole hole bushi* (*bushi* in Japanese means "song" and "hole hole" is what Hawaiians call stripping leaves from dried sugarcane), vividly describes plantation life for these newcomers. "Hawaii, Hawaii," the lyrics read, "Like a dream/So I came/But my tears/Are flowing now/in the canefields."

## Life in the Big City

Hawaii has just one very large city—its capital. The city of Honolulu, on Oahu, has a population of about 337,000. According to the 2010 Census, more than 950,000 Hawaiians live in or around Honolulu. That is about 70 percent of the state's population.

Honolulu is a city of contrasts, with tropical beaches, picturesque historic buildings, and gleaming, modern high-rise buildings. Many businesses are based in Honolulu, providing jobs for its citizens. Honolulu attracts many tourists, whose money helps the local economy. The city has beautiful parks and beaches. Many Honolulu residents complain about the city's traffic congestion and air and water pollution, however.

## Life Away from the Big City

Hawaii's other cities are all much smaller. They include Pearl City, Hilo, Kailua, Kaneohe, Waipahu, Kahului, and Kailua-Kona.

There are still many Hawaiians who live in small villages with little more than a school, a church, a small grocery store, and a post office. In many of these places, people live in old Hawaii-style frame houses with tin roofs.

People who live on Oahu enjoy many of the attractions of big cities. They shop at malls and go to museums, concerts, and theaters. While the other islands are also modern, their cities are not as crowded. Many feel that life on the less-populated islands moves at a slower pace.

### Long Livers

Hawaiians live longer than the residents of any other state. Their life expectancy is 81.5 years, nearly three years longer than the US average of 78.8.

## Education

Missionaries founded the first schools in Hawaii in the 1820s. Then, about twenty years later, King Kamehameha III established a public school system.

Today, Hawaii's school system is unique among the states because it is one statewide system instead of a collection of different school systems run by individual local governments. In 2010, more than 178,000 students attended kindergarten through twelfth grade in 257 regular public schools and 31 charter schools. (Approximately 38,000 students attended private schools in the state.)

The University of Hawaii system has ten campuses on six islands, including seven community colleges. Almost fifty-eight thousand students are enrolled in this educational system. The largest and oldest school in the system is the University of Hawaii at Manoa, located on Oahu. Students there can study for undergraduate, graduate, and professional degrees.

# 10 KEY EVENTS

## 1. International Festival of Canoes

People come from many different Pacific nations to take part in Maui's annual celebration of canoes. At this May event, you can see canoes being carved by master craftspeople or watch canoe races. Drum carving and house thatching are also demonstrated.

## 2. Ironman Triathlon World Championship

Every October, athletes come from around the world to the Big Island to compete in this event. The difficult competition requires participants to swim 2.4 miles (3.8 km) in the ocean, bike for 112 miles (180 km), and run a 26.2-mile (42 km) marathon.

## 3. Kamehameha Festival

This festival is held in June on King Kamehameha Day— Hawaii's oldest state holiday, honoring its first king. Held in Hilo on the Big Island, the festival pays tribute to Hawaiian culture with traditional dance, music, and arts and crafts.

## 4. Kauai Island Crafters Fair

This fair is held every October 25 at the Kauai Veteran's Center. Local artisans and craftspeople display and sell their wares. They make things such as carved bone jewelry, sunrise shell jewelry, quilts, and futons.

## 5. Makawao Rodeo

This is the largest rodeo held in Hawaii. This July event on Maui features paniolo (Hawaiian cowboys) taking part in traditional rodeo events. There is bull roping, steer chasing, bareback riding, country music, and a big parade.

International Festival of Canoes

Ironman Triathlon World Championship

# HAWAII ★ ★ ★ ★

## 6. Merrie Monarch Festival

For almost fifty years, the Hawaii Island Chamber of
Commerce has sponsored the Merrie Monarch Festival on
the Big Island in April to preserve and promote traditional
Hawaiian culture. The highlight is a three-day hula
competition. Dancers prepare months in advance.

## 7. Narcissus Festival

Held in Honolulu in January and February, the Narcissus
Festival is part of the Hawaiian Chinese community's New
Year celebrations. The festival, first held in 1950, includes the
crowning of the Narcissus Queen.

## 8. Prince Kuhio Day

March 26 marks Prince Kuhio Day, a Hawaiian state holiday.
It honors Prince Jonah Kuhio Kalanianaole, who served the
Hawaiian territory as its delegate to the US Congress from
1903 to 1922. Celebrations, including parades, luaus, canoe
races, and festivals are held throughout the state.

## 9. Ukulele Festival

Hundreds of the world's best ukulele players meet in July
to play at the Ukulele Festival in Waikiki. There is even a
performance by a ukulele orchestra made up of eight hundred
musicians, most of them children.

## 10. World Whale Day Celebration

Humpbacks are celebrated at Kalama Park, on Maui, one
Saturday every February as part of the annual Maui Whale
Festival. Thousands of people attend to learn about the
migrating whales as well as to eat, drink, and buy crafts.

Merrie Monarch Festival

Ukulele Festival

The statue shows **THE REVEREND JOSEPH DAMIEN DE VEUSTER, SS. CC.**

## FATHER DAMIEN

**HAWAII**

Father Damien is honored with a statue at the entrance to the Hawaii State Capitol.

# How the Government Works

Like all other states, Hawaii is represented in the US Congress in Washington, DC. Each state has two senators in the US Senate. A state's population determines the number of members it has in the US House of Representatives. States with larger populations have more members. In 2014, Hawaii had two representatives.

Like other US citizens, Hawaiians vote for president every four years. Hawaii also has a state government that works for everybody who lives on the islands.

## County Government

In some ways, Hawaii's government is unlike that of any other state. At the local level, Hawaii has only county governments. Many other states have city and town governments in addition to county governments. County governments in Hawaii take on all the responsibilities usually held by city or town governments in other states. For example, county governments are in charge of fire and emergency medical services, police forces, trash pickup, and street maintenance.

Today, Hawaii has four governmental counties. A fifth county, called Kalawao County, is run by the state health department. Some counties include more than one island. Kalawao County is mostly made up of Kalaupapa National Historical Park, the part

Curved walls grace the chambers of the Hawaii State House of Representatives.

of Molokai to which people with Hansen's disease were sent. The county covers only 52 square miles (134.7 sq km). Also, it has only ninety residents, making it the second smallest county by population in the United States. Loving County, Texas, had only eighty-two residents as of 2010. The rest of Molokai is in Maui County. In Hawaii, it is the counties rather than the cities that have a mayor.

## State Government

Honolulu is Hawaii's state capital. Most of the state government's offices are located there. Because Hawaii is such a new state, it has not had many governors. David Ige was sworn in as the state's eighth governor on December 1, 2014. He replaced Neil Abercrombie, who was elected

## Royal Home

Iolani Palace, the former home of Queen Liliuokalani and her brother King Kalakaua, is the only imperial palace in the United States. It served as Hawaii's government headquarters until 1969. Today, it is a popular tourist attraction.

in 2010 but lost to Ige in 2014 in the Democratic primary for governor. The new lieutenant governor is Shan Tsutsui.

Ige is a descendant of Japanese immigrants. He is the third Asian American to serve as governor of Hawaii. Ige received about half of all votes cast but still won by a comfortable margin. That is because more than forty thousand votes went to Mufi Hannemann, who ran as an independent.

In the past, the governor of the state lived in Queen Liliuokalani's mansion, called Washington Place. In 2002, a new building called the Governor's Residence was completed on the same grounds, and the mansion was turned into a museum.

Hawaii has an unusual state capitol, which was opened in 1969. On the first floor are the chambers of the State Senate and House of Representatives, where the legislators meet. These chambers have walls that curve and slope, similar to cones, to symbolize volcanoes. The capitol also has an open courtyard in the middle, so that people inside the building can look up and see the sun or stars.

Hawaii's state government has three branches—the executive, legislative, and judicial branches—which work to make laws and make sure that the laws are obeyed and interpreted correctly.

Iolani Palace, built in 1882 in Honolulu, has been designated a National Historic Landmark.

# Branches of Government

## Executive

The executive branch enforces state laws. This branch includes the governor, lieutenant governor, attorney general, and state agencies, such as the Department of Health and the Department of Budget and Finance. The governor and lieutenant governor are elected to four-year terms. The governor and lieutenant governor can serve only two terms. The governor appoints the attorney general.

## Legislative

The legislative branch makes state laws. Hawaii's legislature is made up of two chambers, or parts—the State Senate and the State House of Representatives. The senate has twenty-five members. The house of representatives has fifty-one members. Members of the senate are elected to four-year terms. Members of the house of representatives are elected to two-year terms. There is no limit to how many terms a state legislator can serve.

## Judicial

Hawaii's Supreme Court is the highest court in the state. The justices on the supreme court can review state laws to determine whether they agree with or contradict the state constitution. The court has a chief justice and four associate justices. They are nominated by the governor and voted on by the state senate. The second-highest court is the Intermediate Court of Appeals, which is made up of six judges. When a case is decided in a lower court but is appealed, it is the court of appeals that reviews the case to see if it was handled fairly and without error. Decisions by the Intermediate court of appeals can be further appealed to the state supreme court. Like many states, Hawaii also has district courts, trial courts, family courts, and other lower-level courts.

### Silly Law

In Hawaii there is a law that says it is illegal to place coins in one's ears.

# How a Bill Becomes a Law

It takes many steps for a bill to become a law in Hawaii. First, a state senator or member of the State House of Representatives and his or her staff draft a bill and have it introduced in their chamber. The bill is assigned a number. After it is read, the bill is referred to a committee.

**Former governor Neil Abercrombie helped give Hawaii a greener future.**

The committee holds hearings and can choose to change, pass, or reject the bill. A bill that makes it through committee is read for a second and third time in the Senate or House, where members of that chamber can debate it.

Once the bill is passed by a majority vote of the members of the chamber where it was introduced, it is sent to the other chamber. There, it is debated and considered by a committee and voted on again.

If the second chamber passes the bill without changing it, it goes to the governor. But if the second chamber makes changes in the bill, a committee made up of members of both chambers must meet and produce a bill that both chambers can agree on. The final bill is read in both chambers and voted on. If it passes, the bill goes to the governor.

The governor can sign the bill into law or **veto** (reject) it. If the governor vetoes a bill, it can still become law if the house and senate overturn the governor's veto. In order to do this, two-thirds of both houses must vote to override the veto.

## Vote for Green Energy

Before he left office, Governor Abercrombie signed into law a bill that will help families install solar power in their homes. Hawaii is the first state to have such a program, which it calls GEMS (Green Energy Market Securitization).

Under the program, a small fee is added to electric bills of Hawaii residents. The money raised will be used to grant low-interest loans for those who can't get a bank loan or pay early fees for devices such as photovoltaic systems, which convert solar energy into electricity, or energy storage.

State Representative Chris Lee told reporters that the program is targeted at "the middle-to-low-income people who cannot get a big loan from a big bank, but with this financing from the state, will be able to afford solar."

# POLITICAL FIGURES
## FROM HAWAII

## Hiram Fong, US Senator, 1959-1977

Hiram Fong was the son of Chinese parents who came to Hawaii to work on a sugar plantation. He served fourteen years in the territorial House of Representatives and was one of the state's first two senators. He was the first Asian American to be a US senator. He is the only Republican to serve Hawaii in the US Senate.

## Daniel Inouye, US Senator, 1963-2012

Daniel K. Inouye was the first Japanese American ever to serve in the US Congress. Inouye was also a decorated war veteran who lost his right arm in battle during World War II. The highly respected senator from Hawaii was in his seventh term when he died on December 17, 2012, at age eighty-eight.

## Barack Obama, US President, 2009-2017

Barack H. Obama was born in Honolulu in 1961 to a mother from Kansas and a father from Kenya. He spent most of his early years in Hawaii. Obama was elected to the Illinois State Senate and US Senate before being elected the forty-fourth president of the United States in 2008.

# HAWAII
## YOU CAN MAKE A DIFFERENCE

### Contacting Lawmakers

To find contact information for Hawaii's state legislators, go to **www.capitol.hawaii.gov**

There, you can find information about current legislation. In addition, under "Find Legislators," if you type in your address and click "submit," you will be told who your state legislators are.

Volunteers help clean up Kaho'olawe.

### Weapons Test Ban

Kids can make a difference by participating in the law-making process. Study the legislative agenda in your state on either a local or national level and decide if there is an issue you would like to weigh in on. You can use letters or e-mail to contact politicians.

If there is a political issue that you care about, you can make a difference. Many of Hawaii's laws were created because ordinary Hawaiians wanted them.

One example is the movement against bomb testing by the US Navy on the island of Kaho'olawe, which began after the Japanese attack on Pearl Harbor in 1941. Members of a citizens' group Protect Kaho'olawe Ohana (PKO) protested the bombing as dangerous to the environment, historic sites, and the thousands of goats who lived on the island. They occupied the island and filed suit against the navy in a federal court in 1976. As a result, the navy signed an agreement with the group to begin conservation activities on the island in 1980. Ten years later, President George H. W. Bush stopped all bombing on Kaho'olawe. In 1993, Senator Inouye sponsored a bill that would give Kaho'olawe back to Hawaii. Congress then voted to end all military use of the island and authorized $400 million to pay for the removal of ammunition and other military weapons and equipment. The 44.59-square mile (115.5 sq km) island will be used as a place to teach Hawaiian culture and where new generations can learn to be stewards of the land.

Hawaii's main industry is tourism.

# Making a Living

**L**ong before explorers and missionaries came to the islands, Hawaiians had a **subsistence economy**. In other words, they did not make things to sell to other people. Families took care of themselves. They fished, grew crops, and made enough for what they needed. As time went on, different people began to specialize in different skills, such as building houses or boats or carving wood. Individuals also began to barter, or trade, with other people.

By 1800, ships were coming to Hawaii to trade. The people on the ships anchored off Lahaina, on the island of Maui, where they loaded their ships with sandalwood. American whalers began to sail every year to the north Pacific Ocean, hunting whales for their **blubber**. Whale blubber was processed into oil, which was used as fuel for lamps. On their way to the north Pacific, the captains of whaling ships often went to Hawaiian ports to pick up supplies and to allow their sailors to enjoy some time on the shore.

Americans and Europeans first bought land in Hawaii in order to grow sugarcane. Hawaii is an ideal place to raise sugarcane because the crop needs rich soil and a lot of rain. Sugarcane is processed and made into sugar and other goods. Pineapple plantations were also set up to take advantage of the warm, wet weather.

**Hawaiians now consume most of the pineapples grown in the state.**

# Agriculture Today

For a long time, agriculture formed the backbone of the Hawaiian economy. This changed in the twentieth century, when Hawaiians began to make more money from tourism and the military.

Today, the state's largest ranches and plantations are almost all owned by corporations. There are many small farms, though. In 2009, there were 7,500 farms in Hawaii, with an average size of about 150 acres (60 ha). Sugarcane and pineapple are still important crops in Hawaii, even though the state is no longer number one in the world in pineapple packing. In the mid-1950s, Dole Pineapple was the largest pineapple packer in the world and canners in the state employed three thousand people. However, lower labor costs allowed countries with good growing climates, such as Thailand and the Philippines, to produce the fruit for less money. Dole closed its Honolulu cannery in 1991, and Del Monte moved its business in 2008. Most of the four hundred million pineapples farmed in Hawaii today is sold in the state.

Other important agricultural products are other fruits such as bananas and papayas, coffee, seed crops, vegetables including potatoes and cabbage, and flowers. Farms also raise beef cattle, dairy cows, hogs, and chickens (some raised for their meat and some for their eggs).

Smooth-shell macadamia trees were introduced to the islands in the 1880s. Hawaii is famous for the delicious nuts from these trees. Macadamia nuts are among the most nutritious of all nuts. They are also free of gluten, a component of grain flours that some people cannot tolerate, and are a popular ingredient in gluten-free formulas.

# Pacific Waters and Recreation

Some Hawaiians make their living from the water. Many tourists love to fish in Hawaii, and the operators of charter boats earn money by taking people out to fish in the Pacific Ocean. Snorkeling, surfing, and scuba diving are also popular sports. Instructors and stores that rent equipment to tourists can profit from Hawaii's waters.

Spectator sports such as sumo wrestling and football are also popular. Football bowl games have been played in Hawaii since the 1930s, when the Poi Bowl began. Since 2002, the Hawaii Bowl, now called the Sheraton Hawaii Bowl, has been played in December at Aloha Stadium in Honolulu. The Pro Bowl—an all-star game between National Football League players—was held at Aloha Stadium from 1980 to 2009. It returned there in January 2011 for a three-year run and, after a one-year absence, is scheduled to return for the 2016 game.

In December of 2014, Marcus Mariota became the first native of Hawaii to win the Heisman Trophy. That award is given to the top college football player each year. Mariota, a junior quarterback at the University of Oregon, received the second highest possible percentage of points ever in the voting by members of the national media. Mariota is from Honolulu and attended Saint Louis School.

College football teams and NFL all-stars travel to Hawaii to play in Aloha Stadium.

Coffee

Seafood

## 1. Cattle

Hawaii is home to many beef cows, which thrive on the islands' rich grasses. But ranchers have had trouble making much money from their beef because they cannot afford to bring in grain for feed.

## 2. Coffee

Coffee is made from seeds called beans that grow on evergreen trees. Farmers say it is the year-round warm weather, rich volcanic soil, and light winds and rain that make Hawaiian coffee so flavorful.

## 3. Seafood

A few thousand Hawaiians make their living catching fish. Ahi, also called bigeye tuna, and swordfish bring in the most money. There are also more than one hundred aquafarms in Hawaii. They raise shellfish such as shrimp, different kinds of finfish, and seaweed and other sea vegetables.

## 4. Food Processing

Food-processing plants prepare and package food made from crops and animals grown on the islands. One of the most popular processed products is pineapple that is converted into juice, then canned or frozen to be shipped to the mainland.

## 5. Media and Entertainment

Hawaii has been called Hollywood's Tropical Backlot. Among the popular movies shot here are *Jurassic Park* and *Pirates of the Caribbean*. Hawaii has the country's only state-operated film studio. Many TV shows have been shot in Hawaii. *Lost*—which ran from 2004 to 2010—was filmed on Oahu.

# HAWAII ★ ★ ★ ★

Orchids

Sugar

## 6. Military Bases

In 1887, the United States Navy received the exclusive right to use Pearl Harbor as a refueling and repair station for ships in the Pacific. Today, the US Army, Air Force, and Marines also have bases in Hawaii.

## 7. Orchids

Orchids are showy and often sweet-smelling. Hawaii's climate is ideal for these flowers. Many orchids grow wild in Hawaii's natural areas. But orchids are also grown on farms or in greenhouses to be sold to the mainland, Europe, and Asia.

## 8. Pineapple

Pineapples are no longer grown in huge numbers on the islands, but there are still thriving plantations. The Dole Pineapple Plantation is the state's second most popular tourist site.

## 9. Sugar

Sugarcane is a tall grass plant that contains a sweet juice that is processed to become sugar. In 1959, when Hawaii became a state, one out of every twelve Hawaiian workers was in the sugar industry. There are still sugarcane plantations in Hawaii, but the crop is not the moneymaker it once was.

## 10. Tourism

Tourism is Hawaii's biggest industry. In 2012, nearly eight million people visited Hawaii, and most stayed an average of nine days. Most visitors—about 70 percent—come from the United States, although Hawaii is also a popular destination for people from Asia.

# Recipe for Hawaiian Lemonade

In Hawaii, cold fruit drinks are popular any time and season. Follow these instructions to make this delicious lemonade.

## What You Need

6-ounce (177.5-milliliter) can of frozen lemonade concentrate

¾ cup (266 mL) water

12-ounce (355 mL) can unsweetened pineapple juice

12-ounce (355 mL) can apricot nectar

1¼ (238 g) cups ginger ale

lemon slices

ice cubes

a pitcher

## What You Do

- Chill the juice, the nectar, and the ginger ale in the refrigerator. Thaw the frozen lemonade. Then combine the lemonade concentrate and water in a pitcher and stir. Add the nectar and juice. Continue to stir well.
- Let an adult cut the lemon into slices for you.
- Now add the ginger ale, ice cubes, and lemon slices.
- Stir some more and serve to your friends and family. Enjoy this Hawaiian treat!

"In Hawaii, if one person is successful the entire state is successful," Mariota said. "It's family."

## Manufacturing

Manufacturing has never been an important part of Hawaii's economy. Besides food-processing plants, there are few factories. But manufacturing does provide a living for some Hawaiians. Printed materials, metal items, clothing, and textiles are among Hawaii's other manufactured products.

There are also some traditional goods that Hawaiians make and sell to other states or other countries. Hawaii is often associated with the ukulele. Portuguese immigrants who arrived in the late 1800s brought an early version of this little guitar-like instrument to the islands. Hawaiians grew to love the instrument and became skilled at playing and making ukuleles. There are several family-owned ukulele making businesses in Hawaii. Though factories in other states or countries make ukuleles, many musicians and collectors prefer to get their instruments from the Aloha State.

There are a number of theories about how the ukulele got its name. One story says the name means "jumping flea" and relates to the way the instrument is played. To play it, a person needs to move his or her fingers quickly up and down the strings. *Uku* in Hawaiian means "flea," and locals thought that the ukulele player's fast-moving fingers looked like a flea jumping around.

For many Americans, Hawaii is a memorable getaway where they can relax on tropical islands without leaving the country. The wildlife in Hawaii is unlike anywhere on the mainland. Many visitors hike through the forest, see the volcanoes, snorkel or scuba dive along the reefs, or simply relax on the beach. They also enjoy the various cultural events and historic sites.

Visitors who traveled to Hawaii spent $14.3 billion in 2012, a record amount. The state attracted almost eight million visitors that year. A lot of those visitors came from Japan, China, South Korea and other Asian nations, which added a lot of new flights to the islands. Tourism produces more money for the state than any other industry—it was 21 percent of the state's economy in 2012—and helps Hawaii's income in many ways. Hotels, resorts, restaurants, museums, and stores where visitors spend their money employ many Hawaiians. And every time a new hotel is built to house more tourists, people in the construction industry are able to find new jobs.

Tourism has recovered in Hawaii after several years of decline.

## Hawaii's Future

Hawaii has economic problems that its leaders and citizens are trying to address. After the terrorist attacks of September 11, 2001, fewer tourists came to Hawaii, and businesses were hit hard. And when the economy of the United States—and that of the rest of the world—suffers, tourism to Hawaii slows down too. This is what happened beginning in late 2007. However, the economic rebound in the United States revived the tourism industry in Hawaii by 2012, as it returned to or bypassed levels seen before the recession in 2007. However, the economic downturn made it difficult for residents to find jobs. Some decided to move to the mainland, in hopes of better opportunities.

### No Billboards Allowed

It is a state law that billboards cannot be erected in Hawaii. People feel they would mar the state's natural landscape and hurt tourism.

Overall, unemployment is much lower in Hawaii than the average for the rest of the country. The unemployment rate for Hawaii was estimated at 4.2 percent in 2014, the sixth lowest in the nation, and was forecast to drop below 4 percent by 2016. The national average late in 2014 was 5.8 percent.

It is expensive to live in Hawaii. It has the highest cost of living in the United States. Its cost of housing even exceeds New York's. Prices for many goods are always going to be high in Hawaii because they require ships or airplanes to transport them there. These goods include many foods and beverages.

There have been some positive changes in Hawaii's economy. For example, in recent years, there are more and more jobs in health care and construction on the islands. The state is encouraging growth in science and technology, ocean research and development, health and education, tourism, different forms of agriculture, and floral and specialty food products that come only from Hawaii. The clear skies above the volcanoes, Mauna Kea and Haleakala, provide great conditions for astronomers. There are four observatories on Haleakala and thirteen facilities on Mauna Kea. The summit of Mauna Kea hosts the world's largest astronomical observatory, with thirteen working telescopes operated by astronomers from eleven countries.

In addition, Hawaii is a popular location for film and television productions. The state is working to attract even more of these projects. Hawaii would also like to bring more sports events to the state. One of its most successful is the EA Sports Maui Invitational, which brings some of the best college basketball teams to the state for an early season tournament each November. The tournament is hosted each year by Chaminade University, which has turned in some impressive upsets over the years. Twelve teams each year come to Hawaii to play in the Lahaina Civic Center. The tournament began in 1983.

Hawaiians have had to deal with tough times before, and together, the state residents are committed to finding ways to keep the Aloha State's economy as prosperous as possible.

A second version of the television series *Hawaii Five-0* is being filmed on the islands.

# HAWAII
## STATE MAP

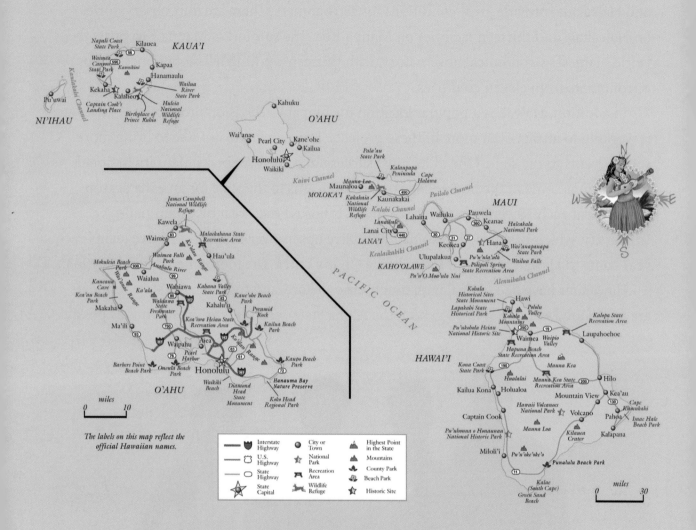

**NI'IHAU**

Pu'uwai

*Kaulakahi Channel*

**KAUA'I**

Napali Coast
State Park
Kilauea
Waimea
Canyon 550
State Park    Kawaikini
Kekaha ★    Kapaa
Kalaheo    Hanamaulu
Captain Cook's    Wailua
Landing Place    River
Birthplace of    State Park
Prince Kuhio    Huleia
National
Wildlife
Refuge

Kahuku

**O'AHU**

Wai'anae    Kane'ohe
Pearl City    Kailua
Honolulu ★
Waikiki

*Kaiwi Channel*

Pala'au
State Park
Kalaupapa
Peninsula    Cape
Halawa
Mauna Loa
Maunaloa    450
**MOLOKA'I**    Kaunakakai    *Pailolo Channel*
Kakahaia
National
Wildlife    Lanaihale
Refuge
Lahaina    Wailuku    **MAUI**
Pauwela
Lanai City    440    Keanae
*Kalohi Channel*    30    Haleakala
**LANA'I**    Keokea    31    National Park
37    Hana
Ulupalakua    Pu'u'ula'ula    Wai'anapanapa
State Park
**KAHO'OLAWE**    Polipoli Spring    Wailua Falls
State Recreation Area
Pu'u'O Moa'ula Nui

*Kealaikahiki Channel*

*PACIFIC OCEAN*

*Alenuihaha Channel*

James Campbell
National Wildlife
Refuge
Kawela
Waimea    83
Malaekahana State
Recreation Area
Waimea Falls    Hau'ula
Park
Mokuleia Beach    Anahulu River
Park    990
Waialua    Ka'ala
Kaneana Cave    80    Wahiawa    Kahana Valley
Kea'au Beach    Wahiawa    State Park    83
Park    State    Kane'ohe
Makaha    Freshwater    Beach
Park    Park
Ma'ili    Kea'iwa Heiau State    Pyramid
Recreation Area    Rock
750    Kailua Beach
Park
93    H1
Waipahu    Aiea
Barbers Point    Pearl    63
Beach Park    78    Harbor    61    Kaupo Beach
Oneula Beach    Park
Park    **Honolulu**
Waikiki    72
Beach    Diamond    Hanauma Bay
Head    Nature Preserve
**O'AHU**    State
Monument    Koko Head
Regional Park

*miles*
0    10

*The labels on this map reflect the
official Hawaiian names.*

**HAWAI'I**

Kohala
Historical Sites
State Monument    Hawi
Lapakahi State    Pololu
Historical Park    Valley
Kohala
Mountains    Kalopa State
Pu'ukohola Heiau    295    Recreation Area
National Historic Site    19    Waimea    Laupahoehoe
Hapuna Beach    Waipio
State Recreation Area    Valley
Kona Coast    190    Mauna Kea
State Park    Hualalai    Mauna Kea State
Recreation Area    200    Hilo
Kailua Kona    Holualoa    Mountain View    Kea'au
Cape
Captain Cook    Volcano    130    Kumukahi
Pahoa    Inae Hale
Hawaii Volcanoes    Mauna Loa    Beach Park
National Park    Kilauea
Pu'uhonua o Honaunau    Crater    Kalapana
National Historic Park
Miloli'i    Pu'u'oke'oke'o    11    Punalulu Beach Park
Kalae
(South Cape)
Green Sand
Beach    *miles*
0    30

### Legend

| | Interstate Highway | ● | City or Town | ▲ | Highest Point in the State |
|---|---|---|---|---|---|
| | U.S. Highway | ⬟ | National Park | ▲ | Mountains |
| | State Highway | ○ | Recreation Area | | County Park |
| ★ | State Capital | | Wildlife Refuge | | Beach Park |
| | | | | ★ | Historic Site |

# HAWAII
## MAP SKILLS

1. What is the highest point on Kauai?

2. On what island is the state capital of Honolulu found?

3. What is the northernmost town on the island of Hawaii?

4. Which island lies between Maui and Molokai?

5. What state recreation area is located on Maui?

6. What national park is located on the island of Hawaii?

7. What interstate highway runs north from Diamond Head on Oahu?

8. Which National Wildlife Refuge is found in southern Kauai?

9. What body of water in the Pacific Ocean lies between Molokai and Oahu?

10. Which is the most westerly Hawaiian island shown on this map?

Kawaikini Peak

Lanai

10. Niihau
9. Kaiwi Channel
8. Huleia
7. Interstate H1
6. Hawaii Volcanoes National Park
5. Polipoli Springs
4. Lanai
3. Hawi
2. Oahu
1. Kawaikini

# State Flag, Seal, and Song

Hawaii's flag has the Union Jack—the flag of Great Britain—in its upper left–hand corner. The Union Jack appears because British explorer George Vancouver gave the British flag to King Kamehameha I as a gift. At the time, Kamehameha was bringing together the islands, and he decided to use the Union Jack as Hawaii's unofficial flag. Eventually, in 1816, eight red, white, and blue stripes were added to symbolize the eight main islands.

In the center of the seal is a design based on the royal coat of arms of the Kingdom of Hawaii. King Kamehameha I is shown holding a staff, and the Goddess of Liberty is shown holding the Hawaiian flag. The seal also has many symbols including a tabu ball and stick, which stand for the power of the government. The seal also features eight taro leaves, a phoenix, and a star. The top of the seal has the words "State of Hawaii" and the year the state joined the union. The state's motto ("The life of the land is perpetuated in righteousness") is on the bottom.

The state song is "Hawaii Ponoi" with words by King David Kalakaua and music by Henry Berger. It was written in 1876 to honor King Kamehameha I. To see the lyrics in Hawaiian and English, and listen to the song, visit: **www.50states.com/songs/hawaii.htm#.VFKPNVfp_B0**.

# Glossary

**annexation**    The taking over of territory by another country or state.

**archipelago**    A large chain of islands grouped together.

**blubber**    A layer of fat beneath the skin of whales and other large sea mammals.

**ecosystem**    A natural area where living organisms—plants and animals—interact.

**geologists**    Scientists who study Earth's structure and history.

**isthmus**    A narrow strip of land that is bordered on both sides by water and connects two larger bodies of land.

**leis**    Strings of flowers given to visitors and to other people on special occasions.

**leprosy**    A contagious disease that causes skin lesions and damage to the nerves, muscles, and eyes.

**luaus**    Traditional Hawaiian feasts that usually feature poi and a roasted pig.

**magma**    Hot, melted rock beneath Earth's crust that sometime rises to the surface.

**missionaries**    People who travel to new lands to convert the natives to their religion.

**Polynesian**    A race of people who live on islands in the central and south Pacific Ocean.

**subsistence economy**    A way of life where people exist on what they can provide for themselves with little or nothing left over to sell to others.

**veto**    To reject a bill or law in government that has been legally passed.

# More About Hawaii

## BOOKS

Carolan, Dr. Terry, and Joanna Carolan. *A President from Hawaii*. Hanapepe, HI: Banana Patch Press, 2009.

Dyan, Penelope. *Yesterday's Rain – A Kids' Guide to Kauai, Hawaii*. Jamul, CA: Bellissima Publishing, 2013.

Feinstein, Stephen. *Hawai'i Volcanoes National Park: Adventure, Explore, Discover*. Berkeley Heights, NJ: MyReportLinks.com Books, 2009.

Mattern, Joanne. *Hawaii: Past and Present*. New York: Rosen Central, 2010.

## WEBSITES

**HawaiiHistory.org**
www.hawaiihistory.org

**Hawaii's Official State Website**
www.ehawaii.gov

**Hawaii's Official Tourism Site**
www.gohawaii.com

## ABOUT THE AUTHORS

**Steven Otfinoski** has written more than 160 books for young readers, including many state books. He spent one memorable Christmas vacation with his family on the island of Kauai.

**Ann Graham Gaines** lives with her children deep in the woods of Texas. For close to twenty years, she has been writing children's nonfiction books and doing picture research.

**Jacqueline Laks Gorman** has been a writer and editor for approximately thirty years. She was raised in New York and moved to the Midwest in the 1990s. She and her family live in DeKalb, Illinois.

# Index

Page numbers in **boldface** are illustrations. Entries in **boldface** are glossary terms.

# Index